Learning a Joy

EDITED BY JIM LARSON

G/L REGAL BOOKS

A Division of G/L Publications
Glendale, California, U.S.A.

Scripture quotations used in this book
are from the:
NASB New American Standard Bible. © The Lockman
Foundation, 1971. Used by permission.
TLB The Living Bible, Paraphrased (Wheaton:
Tyndale House, Publishers, 1971). Used by
permission.

Published by
Regal Books Division, G/L Publications
Glendale, California 91209, U.S.A.

ISBN 0-8307-0362-4

CONTENTS

# PREFACE

Children around the world are discovering the wonder of God's love and the value of His truth for their lives through the means of effective teaching and learning in the Sunday School. The purpose of this book is to provide a concise summary of important guidelines for both department leaders and teachers of elementary-age children in the Sunday School. If your reading and discussion of this book with your fellow teachers and leaders gives you a better understanding of your responsibility and broadens your vision of what *can* be done, the purpose of this book has been accomplished.

I would especially like to thank Ruth Bathauer, Frances Blankenbaker, Diane Wheatley, Carol Noren and Sheryl Hamstad for developing the Bible learning resources which were so essential to the writing of this book.

May God guide you as you sharpen your skills to become an increasingly effective teacher—a guide and a facilitator in the learning of God's Word and the reflection of His love.

Jim Larson
Editor

Chapter One
TEND THE FLOCK OF GOD

As a teacher or leader of children in the Sunday School, there are probably many important questions you have—about schedule, job descriptions, the use of Bible learning activities, worship, and many more. Before we discuss these concerns, we want to emphasize the high calling God has given you as you minister to children.

The apostle Peter exhorted church leaders many centuries ago with a challenge which all of us need to take to heart:

"Feed the flock of God; care for it willingly, not grudgingly; not for what you will get out of it, but because you are eager to serve the Lord. Don't be tyrants, but lead them by your good example, and when the Head Shepherd comes, your reward will be a never-ending share in his glory and honor" (1 Pet. 5:2-4, *TLB*).

Let's look at a few key thoughts in this challenge:

Feed the flock of God. Another translation uses the word "tend," which implies not only the feeding of the sheep but the whole of

2

the shepherd's care for his flock. As leaders and teachers of children, God wants us to be concerned about the total welfare of our children—with their physical, emotional, intellectual and spiritual concerns. With the good news of Jesus and our loving concern, we must provide them with a diet of good food—vital truths of Scripture which can be translated into the everyday experiences of each child.

Note that Peter calls people "the flock of God." These are God's children, not our own. God has given us these people and wants us to honor and cherish them. Obviously, this is a great responsibility, but it is also a great privilege. God has called us to be the human agents through which He expresses His love to people everywhere.

Peter focuses on the importance of our attitudes as well. There is a great difference between doing work because we have to (being grim, resentful or seeing the job as a burden) and seeing it as an opportunity for serving God. Children easily discern our attitudes, whether they be positive or negative. A positive, enthusiastic attitude will greatly enhance your ministry. Ask God to give you the kind of attitude which will help make you an effective Christian leader.

The apostle also mentions that we should not be leaders for what we can get out of it. There is a fine line between serving as a Christian educator because we want to serve God and reach children for Christ, and doing it to meet our own needs. If the latter is true, a temptation to treat people as objects rather than as unique creations of God arises. We are servants and leaders of children. We are not to be policemen or authoritarian despots seeking to control them. If our service comes from pure wellsprings of love for God and for the children, we will see growth and change in their lives. If our attitudes and motives are bitter or negative, growth will probably not be as great a possibility.

Notice in verse 3 the great importance of being examples. Peter says, *Lead them by your good example.* The root of the word "example" means "pattern" or "model," that from which casts or copies are taken. Children have heroes. The question is what kind of heroes will they be. Do you want the children in your Sunday School to imitate the attitudes and actions we exhibit?

People can be led only as far as we are willing to take them. We lead on the basis of what we have personally experienced for ourselves. Our own personal growth thus becomes a vital necessity. If we are stagnant, our group will probably be the same. If we are dynamic and enthusiastic, so will our group be.

The goal of our work, as expressed in verse 4, is the approval by the Head Shepherd. We may become discouraged at times with the seeming lack of interest on the part of some children, or lack the wisdom in how to channel the endless amounts of energy they possess. Maybe you're worrying about not "getting through" to the children, or not having an adequate amount of preparation time for Sundays. Whatever your concerns, remember the promise Peter makes in verse 4: when Christ returns, He will reward you with a *never-ending share in his glory and honor.* God knows what you are attempting to do right now for children—of your concerns, your efforts to share His love with them. He knows your strengths as well as your weaknesses, and He appreciates all you are doing for Him. Your ultimate reward will be eternal fellowship with Him. In the meantime, be joyful when you see responses from your children—the excitement of learning through discovery; an awakening interest in spiritual matters; a growth in your relationships with the children; opportunities to reach out in love to their families.

God has promised to give us all that we need to accomplish the mission He has called us to do. Ask Him for the strength, wisdom and love to care for God's children by guiding them to become members of His family and grow to maturity as His children.

Check Yourself

1. Define what Peter means by "feed the flock of God." List specific ways you can implement this challenge in your Sunday School.

2. Identify how a leader's attitude affects his students. Why is a positive attitude essential?

3. Read 1 Peter 5:2-4 again. Write these verses in your own words. Which of Peter's commands is most difficult for you to obey? Commit this need to God. Thank Him for His love.

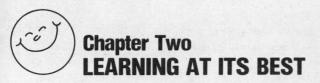

Chapter Two
LEARNING AT ITS BEST

God's Word reminds us that "a wise teacher makes learning a joy" (Prov. 15:2, *TLB*). You have at your disposal today many methods and tools which can make the study of God's Word a joy for both you and your children. What an exciting time to be teaching children!

In past decades Christian educators have focused primarily on teaching—on teacher education and instructional techniques. But now the focus is rightfully turning toward an emphasis on learning. One of the wise teacher's primary concerns is first—how does the child learn? Then—how can I best help the child to learn?

How Do Children Learn?

Children Learn Through Their Five Senses

Children are by nature inquisitive. Their eyes must see, their ears hear and their hands move. When children are involved in using learning resources for their Bible study, their interest and joy in learning grows. Their involvement in Bible research projects, Bible discovery games and other creative Bible learning activities can make Bible facts and principles understandable and applicable for children.

Children Learn Through Experiences

Words are abstract until experiences help to give them meaning. Remember that children have relatively few years of experience upon which to base their discussion of Bible truths. So children learn best by doing—by participating in experiences which allow them to practice the new behavior or principle the teacher guides them to understand.

Children Learn Through a Variety of Methods

Writing, singing, drawing, memorizing, telling and dramatizing are all valuable means through which children can discover important Christian principles for daily living. Some methods work better for some children than others. Variety in methods will help to make learning a joy for your children.

Children Learn at Different Rates

The effective teacher avoids making a child feel guilty for his short attention span or slow working habits. The wise teacher finds special ways to encourage those who work slowly and provides special challenges for those who work quickly. He plans ways to adjust his schedule and activities to meet the needs of each child.

Children Learn Through Many People

Children learn through one teacher, several teachers, other children and by themselves. Children need to talk and work together in the learning process. From such interaction can come valuable impromptu lessons. For example, as children are working together there may be opportunities to guide them to put into practice Bible truths such as "show love one to another" and "in honor preferring one another." The wise teacher guides the child in discovering immediate ways to apply Bible principles to his own life.

Children Learn Best When They Feel Successful

Children profit most from projects and assignments which are within their ability and thus build a sense of confidence. A teacher's warm, honest praise as children work also encourages and reinforces meaningful learning. A spirit of competition among children who are naturally diverse in their abilities, their rate of learning and comprehension level, often hinders effective learning. The best kind of Bible learning is that which causes every child to feel some sense of accomplishment.

Children Learn Best What Is Meaningful to Them

Knowing Bible facts and memorizing Scripture are important, but there is much more than facts and memorization to effective Bible learning. Children need additional challenges if they are to understand that God's Word speaks to their own everyday experiences. Therefore, the wise teacher guides children through a variety of Bible learning experiences which help to clarify biblical facts and truths. To these the Holy Spirit adds understanding and prompts changes of attitudes and actions—the real evidence of Bible learning.

Learning Through Discovery Is Best!

What these seven basic teaching/learning principles say in summary is that children learn best by becoming actively involved in discovering information and truths which have meaning for them. Children involved in learning what God's Word says to them need patterns, and opportunities to practice doing what Scripture teaches. Learning through discovery creates the possibility for effective Bible learning to take place during the Sunday School session—as well as throughout the week.

How Can Bible Learning Activities Help?

Children in the Sunday School respond positively to Bible learning projects or activities which illustrate and enrich the Bible truths being studied. Bible learning activities help the learner (1) review Bible information; (2) apply Bible truths to his own life; and (3) develop skills in using the Bible and other research materials. Bible learning activities do much to make learning a joyful experience.

Bible Learning Activities Differ from Craft Projects

A craft project may provide an interesting and profitable learning experience, but neither the process nor the product necessarily increases Bible knowledge or understanding of ways to apply Scripture truth to everyday living.

Bible learning activities, on the other hand, are always related to biblical facts or application to life. Bible learning activities also focus on the Scriptures being studied each Sunday within the unit.

Here are some distinguishing features of valid Bible learning activities:

1. They require research (using Bible, other resources).

2. They involve children in problem solving and/or decision-making as to how to share what they learned.

3. They provide opportunities for children to make choices, accept responsibility and work together.

4. They promote creative thinking when a teacher guides children to think and plan for themselves.

5. They give students opportunities to express what they know;

give teachers opportunities to evaluate children's learning and correct any misconceptions.

6. They provide opportunity for children to talk with each other and with the teacher, an essential part of the learning process.

Choice Is an Important Part of Meaningful Learning

Children have different interests and abilities. Some may learn best from art projects; others may profit more from music or research projects. Therefore, children need the opportunity to choose Bible learning experiences which interest them most. Also, their making choices helps them develop ability and self-confidence needed to make decisions in other matters of life.

To Summarize . . .

Are you providing valid Bible learning experiences which make learning a joy for your children? Learning through involvement and discovery will help make the Bible come alive for your children. When learning is a joy for your children, teaching will become a joy for you as well!

Check Yourself

1. List at least five facts you have discovered about how children learn.

2. Define the term "Bible learning activity." List distinguishing features of valid Bible learning activities. How are Bible learning activities different from craft projects?

3. Why is choice an important part of meaningful learning?

For Further Reading

(See chapter 12 for information on these books.)

Ways to Plan and Organize (chapters 1,2) provides basic principles for understanding the learning process.

Ways to Help Them Learn gives an excellent analysis of the child as learner (chapter 4), the importance of Bible learning activities (chapter 8), and descriptions of such activities as research, art, drama and music for effective implementation (chapters 9-14).

Bible Learning Activities describes the teaching pattern of Jesus and the learning process (chapters 1-3) and provides guidelines for the use of Bible games (chapter 8).

Chapter Three
TWO WAYS TO SCHEDULE YOUR SUNDAY SCHOOL TIME

Perhaps you're wondering how to implement Bible Learning Activities into your present schedule. Here are two schedules which

PLAN B

1

BIBLE STUDY
(Early Time + 25 minutes)
Building Bible Readiness: Activities to build readiness for Bible story.
Exploring God's Word: Presentation of visualized Bible story.
Living God's Way: Relationship of Bible truths to day-by-day experiences.

BIBLE LEARNING ACTIVITIES
(20 minutes)
Creative activities to reinforce Bible truths.

2

BIBLE SHARING
(15-20 minutes)
Moments of Worship: Songs, offering, prayer and varied worship activities related to lesson/unit aims.
(On the last Sunday of each unit, allow additional time for children to share Bible Learning Activities from previous Sundays of the unit.)

many churches have used successfully for creative Bible teaching/learning in the Sunday School. Each plan allows for Bible Study, Bible Learning Activities and worship.

PLAN A

1

BIBLE STUDY
(Early Time + 25-35 minutes)

Building Bible Readiness: Activities to build readiness for Bible story.
Exploring God's Word: Presentation of visualized Bible story.
Living God's Way: Relationship of Bible truths to day-by-day experiences.

2

BIBLE SHARING
(10-15 minutes)

Moments of Worship: Songs, offering, prayer and varied worship activities related to lesson/unit aims.
Choosing Bible Learning Activities: Procedure by which each child chooses a Bible Learning Activity.

3

BIBLE LEARNING ACTIVITIES
(20-25 minutes)

Creative activities to reinforce Bible truths. Each child works in the Bible Learning Activity group he chose for the unit. (On last Sunday of unit, reverse steps 2 and 3 to allow additional time for Bible Sharing as children present what they learned in activities.)

How to Choose the Best Plan for You

Consider choosing PLAN B if . . .

You have more than two grades in a department and ten or less enrolled.

You cannot arrange your time schedule into three blocks of time. Consider choosing PLAN A if . . .

You use closely graded curriculum—a department for each school grade.

You have two grades together in a department—such as grades 1 and 2, grades 3 and 4, or 5 and 6. (Until you can have a single grade in each department, you may cycle the material using grade 3 one year and grade 4 the next, etc.)

You have ten or more children in a department.

You have space for students to meet in one large group and in two or more small groups.

Here's How to Get Started

1. Start by using Plan B schedule. Introduce only one new step at a time. For example, you might start by providing Bible Readiness activities from which children choose when they arrive.

Begin by using only one or two Bible Readiness choices each Sunday.*

Then add another of the suggested choices, but make sure that at least one of them is an independent activity—one which children can do on their own without your direct help (e.g., a Bible learning game with which children are already familiar).

You never need to provide *all* the choices suggested in your Teacher's Manual. Rather CHOOSE and ADAPT those which best fit *your* situation.

Help children learn to work independently (1) by providing simple instructions written on stand-up cards (made from parts of file folders or large index cards) or for non-readers, by providing instructions on a cassette tape; (2) by having all supplies readily available; (3)

*See the Bible Readiness suggestions in each lesson of your G/L Teacher's Manual.

by storing in a special place Bible learning games from which children may choose as they complete other readiness activities.

2. When you and the children are comfortable with using Bible Readiness choices at the *beginning* of your class time, start using a Bible learning activity toward the *end* of your class time. You and/or children choose which activity to work on.

When you and the children are comfortable with using Bible learning activities in class time, consider the possibility of letting children choose Bible learning activity groups as in Plan A. If you choose to follow Plan A, change your schedule to include the three blocks of time suggested on chart above.

Questions You May Be Asking . . .

1. Why should we arrange our time schedule so that the large group time comes after class time—as in Plans A and B?

There are several reasons why you'll find this to be the most effective way of planning your Sunday School schedule.

(a) The Building Readiness choices are planned to lead right into the Bible story. At appropriate times during Exploring God's Word (class time) the children share information and Bible verses they worked on in their Building Readiness choices. Therefore it is important that the large group time not interrupt the natural flow from Building Readiness choices to Exploring God's Word.

(b) The children are better able to give attention to Bible Study at the beginning of the hour.

(c) The large group time is planned to reinforce and build on what was studied during Bible Study (class) time. The Bible truths emphasized in Bible Study time prepare the children for a time of meaningful worship in the large group.

2. Our pianist comes during the first part of the hour and then goes to an adult class. How can we plan for music if we have the large group at the middle or end of the hour?

There are several possibilities:

(a) Encourage your pianist to become a full-time member of your department staff. If he does not wish to be responsible for a class group, he can assist staff with Building Readiness and Bible learning activities, be available to counsel or work with individual students as needed, assist the secretary, be in charge of supplies.

(b) Or, ask your pianist to put the songs for each unit on a cassette tape. Then use the cassette tape as your accompaniment for singing.

(c) Or, staff members or children can learn to use an autoharp as accompaniment for singing. (Very simple to use.)

(d) Or, let children sing without accompaniment if a staff member with a definite sense of pitch and rhythm begins the song and sings along with children and teachers.

(e) Or, ask someone who plays a guitar to accompany singing.

Check Yourself

1. List and describe the two main parts of the Plan B schedule and the three main parts of the Plan A schedule.
2. Would Plan A or Plan B best fit your situation? What steps would you need to take to use Plan A or B? How would you begin?

For Further Reading

(See chapter 12 for information on these books.)

Ways to Plan and Organize (chapter 3) provides more details on how to make the best use of time in Sunday School.

Bible Learning Activities (chapter 7) describes the values of both small and large groups and suggests ways to use both size groups profitably.

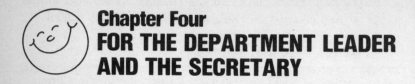

Chapter Four
FOR THE DEPARTMENT LEADER
AND THE SECRETARY

IF YOU ARE THE DEPARTMENT LEADER

What an important responsibility you have as the leader of a children's department in your Sunday School! You are the key person on your teaching team. You are a leader and teacher of both teachers and children. If you are helping children study God's Word effectively, being the department leader is an exceedingly important responsibility.

Maybe you've been wondering about what you should be doing as the leader. Perhaps you'd like some specifics. Here is a checklist of ways you can be an effective and successful leader, with God's help.

How Do You Fit into the Total Church Program?

As one of your church's Sunday School leaders, you will:
• Work within the framework of church policy in recruiting and recommending personnel for your department.
• Help your department teachers and other staff members understand and fulfill their assignments.
• Consult frequently with the general Sunday School superintendent, or the person otherwise designated by the Board of Christian Education, to share information, needs and plans.
• Keep the church leadership informed of the progress and needs of your department. Share information about new contacts, illness or other needs in families of students.

● Evaluate the space and equipment in your department with your staff and share these needs with the Sunday School superintendent or the person assigned responsibility for these matters.

● Participate in your church's program of outreach in order to find those in your area who are not enrolled in the Sunday School.

How Do You Work with Your Staff?

● Remember, you and your staff are learners together in Christ.

● Know your staff as individuals and pray regularly for each one.

● Promote a team spirit. Think and pray about ways to build team unity. Work to build confidence and trust among your staff members. Be sincere in your help and praise as you work with your staff. As teachers sense your care for them individually and as they learn to care for and trust one another they will share their needs and ideas. Sharing and praying together will help build strong team unity.

● Encourage staff members to affirm each other. For example, you may have them share one quality they genuinely appreciate in a fellow staff member. Affirmation such as "I appreciate Mr. A's promptness" or "Miss B's sincere concern for others has been a real help to me" does wonders for team spirit!

● Look for success and encourage staff frequently. As each member feels a measure of success, you, too, will experience success.

● Listen carefully when a discouraged teacher comes to you. Listen prayerfully. (Resist any impulse to lecture!) Repeat what you think you heard the teacher say—such as "You feel this work is not worth the effort." Give the teacher an opportunity to "hear" what he is saying and to decide if that is what he really means. Ask questions. Let him talk. Often a troubled teacher solves his own problem as he shares it with an interested, sympathetic listener.

● Be a spiritual leader to your staff. This doesn't mean a "superior" Christian, but rather a committed, consistent one. Lean heavily upon the Lord and keep in touch with Him daily.

● Study ways to help you build spiritual and team unity. Consider a personal or group study of the Regal paperbacks, *Lord, Make My Life a Miracle* by Raymond C. Ortlund, or *Body Life* by Ray

C. Stedman (G/L Publications, Glendale, California). A discussion guide is also available for the study of *Body Life*.

● Plan and lead regular monthly staff meetings to organize plans for each unit and share mutual needs.

After a year of planning and using new ideas for the total Sunday School hour, one department leader said, "You know, the department leader is really the key! In fact, as goes the leader, so goes the entire department!" How true! Department leader, *you* are a very important person!

How Should You Plan Staff Meetings?

● Schedule a staff meeting on a regular monthly basis.

● Become thoroughly acquainted with the Bible curriculum by reading through the course introduction in the Teacher's Manual to discover the overall purpose and content of the course.

● Read the unit introduction. Note especially the unit aims. (A unit, remember, is a group of lessons related to one theme.) Note how each lesson aim will help you accomplish the unit aim.

● Plan for participation by staff at the meeting by giving assignments to various members—reading and reporting on suggested articles in the Teacher's Manual, demonstrating use of Teaching Resources, etc.

● Encourage each teacher to read through the Bible Learning Activities suggested for the unit in the Teacher's Manual and be ready to indicate a first and second choice of activities he will prepare to lead throughout the unit.

● Check with your pastor or church office for the Sunday School and church calendar of special events for the next two months. Duplicate enough copies for each staff member; or post dates on poster or chalkboard for each to copy.

How Should You Lead Staff Meetings?

● Your job is to lead, facilitate and delegate—but not to dominate nor do most of the talking at a staff meeting.

● Encourage teachers to know their students personally through observation, informal chats, phone calls, and other contacts. Know the children yourself.

● Develop and maintain a plan in which your staff members effectively enlist the cooperation of the students' parents in understanding the purpose of the Sunday School's ministry.

● Guide staff in becoming familiar with the *unit* aims and the *lesson* aims in the effort to use the curriculum more effectively.

● Discuss the Bible Learning Activities for the unit with your teachers. Determine who will lead each activity.

● Look at the suggested unit songs and notice how they will help to reinforce the unit and lesson aims. Learn the songs by singing them together several times.

● Be sure staff understands the department plans for sharing the Bible Learning Activities at the end of the unit.

● Include time for sharing and Bible reading together. (The Scripture portion for the first lesson of the unit would be an appropriate study.) Encourage staff members to share their blessings and needs. You may need to share briefly first, then invite others to share their thoughts and responses to the Scripture selected. Sharing from the Word can do much to reinforce and unify your departmental team. Spend time then praying for each other.

● Plan a calendar of any special events during the coming few months. Coordinate your planning with overall church calendar you have duplicated or posted.

What Do You Do on Sunday Morning?

Even when you are not leading the total group, your role is still to coordinate and be the key leader of the department. Each Sunday morning you should arrive early to make sure the room and materials are ready, and to greet the first students and staff members.

During Bible Study (first block of time in Plans A and B)
● Be ready to help teachers as they arrive. Do they have all needed supplies for readiness activities and Bible study?

● Give last minute instructions to the substitute teacher and introduce him to his class.

- Greet parents with new students and briefly explain the program of Bible Study. Either you or the secretary assigns new students to their classes.
- Walk with a new student to his class, introduce him to the teacher, who will introduce him to other class members.
- Watch for students who arrive a bit late and direct them to their proper groups.
- Work with teachers who may have students displaying behavior problems. Remember, you and your teachers are team members. You will not take away a teacher's responsibility, but will assist him by perhaps working with an individual child who is creating a problem. At times, you may want to take the child out of the group and work individually with him.
- Observe class groups.
- Be alert also for opportunities to assist teachers by counseling a child who is ready to believe in the Lord Jesus as his Saviour. Use the booklet, "God Wants YOU to Be a Member of His Family"* and guide child to think through the suggested Scripture verses. Pray with the child as he believes in Jesus Christ as his Saviour. Give the child his own copy of the booklet to help him remember his decision and to share it with his parents and friends.

During Bible Sharing (the second block of time in Plan A, the last block of time in Plan B)
- Give signal to assemble after a few minutes' warning.
- Seek to create a meaningful learning and worship experience by using songs, Scripture and prayer with only brief reference to biblical facts or principles expressed in lesson.
- If you are using Plan A, guide students in selecting the Bible Learning Activities (BLA) at the beginning of each unit. Enthusiastically introduce each BLA your staff has selected. Give brief highlights of what students can expect to do in each activity. Example: "This is a fun-to-do activity. Some of you will make puppets, others will write a script, and some of you will make the stage." Do not give the name of teacher who will lead activity until *after* all the

*Available from your regular church supplier.

children have made their choices. A child should choose an activity he enjoys rather than choosing to be with his favorite teacher. Limit size of BLA groups to 6–8. Encourage children to have second choice in mind in case they don't get their first choices.

• Be sure to make list of students and the activities they choose for your own records. Post list so all may see.

• From week to week students may check the bulletin board to be reminded of the activity group to which they belong.

• After the worship moments of sharing on the second Sunday of a unit, dismiss children to their respective activities. Ask new students and those absent last week to remain in the large group. Then follow the same procedure of the previous week in letting these students select from activities which still have room for more children.

• For the last lesson of a unit, the schedule is changed in Plan A. Students go directly from Bible Study groups to BLA groups. Use a predetermined signal, such as a bell or piano chord. Remind students that they are to go to their activity groups and complete plans for sharing the learning activities they have been working on during the past Sundays.

• In the Sharing time, on the last Sunday of a unit, lead students and teachers in sharing the BLA they worked on together. Keep this sharing time interesting and meaningful. To add variety, intersperse unit songs, prayer, Bible verses and offering between times of sharing.

During Bible Learning Activities (the third block of time in Plan A, included with Bible Study in Plan B)

• Be alert for any problems which arise, or any student who for some reason has become detached from his activity group.

• Check on supplies. Supplies for children should be available so that one student from each group might be appointed by his teacher to get the supplies for his BLA group and take them to his area. (Or, to save time, supplies may be distributed before BLA time.)

• Give whatever assistance a BLA leader (teacher) might ask for, such as helping a slow student or guiding those who may become sidetracked back to their activities. Remember: this is a busy time with everyone actively involved. Expect a level of "busy noise" which is necessary when groups are planning and working together.

What Are Some Ways to Recognize Birthdays?

Recognizing a child's birthday is important. It says, "I care about you and I want to share in the times that are important to you." However, it is also important not to use the brief Bible learning time for this recognition. As a staff, consider: (1) sending a birthday card in the mail and telephoning a child on his birthday; (2) taking a small cake to the child's home on his birthday; (3) giving a child a birthday pin as he arrives on Sunday morning and having a "special" birthday chair for him in the Sharing time.

How Can You Welcome Visitors?

This part of your program needs to be planned so it does not use important Bible learning time. Some visitors feel uncomfortable about being the center of attention during large group time. So it may be better to welcome each visitor in a special way as he arrives. The teacher, in turn, may plan for one or two children to be special friends who stay with the visitor throughout the Sunday School period. Continue to make the visitor feel welcome by contacting him during the week by phone, visit or card.

How Should You Collect the Offering?

As children arrive, have them put offering in container at love-gift center (e.g., near a poster that says, "God loves a cheerful giver," 2 Cor. 9:7). Place love-gift center far enough from door so children don't feel they are "paying to get in." Ask a child to bring offering to the front for offering prayer during Bible Sharing time. This plan has the same teaching/worship value as passing offering plates, but it takes less time.

IF YOU ARE THE DEPARTMENT SECRETARY

• Be a warm and friendly person who greets children as they arrive.

• Assist department leader in taking new children to their assigned groups.

• Keep accurate attendance records and determine ways to improve the follow-up ministry.

• Record offering and give it to the proper person.

• Assist in ordering and maintaining supplies and curriculum.

• Assist leader by making notes of staff meeting plans, especially the designation of responsibilities; and by reminding teachers of the special tasks agreed upon.

As secretary, you are an important person on the departmental team. Your assistance to the department leader and teachers will help make your church's ministry with children an efficient and joyful experience for everyone.

Check Yourself

1. Identify at least four ways the department leader plays a key role in the total church program.

2. List specific ways the department leader can promote a team spirit and minister to members of his staff.

3. What are the specific duties for the department leader during each of these activities:

Bible Study
Bible Sharing
Bible Learning Activities

4. How is the secretary an important part of the department team effort?

For Further Reading

Ways to Plan and Organize (chapter 5) provides excellent descriptions of leadership roles.

Ways to Help Them Learn (chapter 7) gives additional helps for staff planning, as does *Ways to Plan and Organize* (chapter 7).

Chapter Five
FOR THE TEACHER

As a teacher of a small group of children, you have an exciting opportunity to teach Bible truths and guide your group to discover what God's Word says for their lives today.

Perhaps you are wondering what your responsibilities are. Here is a brief description of your role as teacher.

During Bible Study

- Meet with permanent class group.
- Establish a warm and friendly classroom atmosphere by knowing each of your students and his family.
- Guide Readiness activities so that Bible learning begins the moment your first student arrives.
- Guide Bible Study.
- Help students apply Scripture truths to their lives.
- Guide students to further understanding through their involvement in pages of their student books.
- Encourage students to memorize with understanding their weekly Bible verses.
- Help each child sense his personal importance to you, and to the Lord.

● Provide opportunities for each child to talk with you about what it means to believe in Jesus Christ as his Saviour. Be sensitive to the Holy Spirit's leading. Never require a decision, but give opportunity for child to respond by believing in the Saviour now, or to come and talk with you later about what it means to become a member of God's forever family. Read through the booklet, *God Wants You to Be a Member of His Family*, with the child.

During Bible Sharing

● Assist department leader in leading worship time.
● Sit with and worship with the children.

During Bible Learning Activities

● Lead activity group in Bible research and creative activities to reinforce Bible truths. You will lead a new activity each unit.

During the Week

● Pray for each student.
● Contact absentees as well as regular attenders. (See next chapter for specific ideas on how to build relationships with children.)
● Be a dependable member of your department team by attending planning meetings regularly, consulting with other teachers or the leader; also, by caring and praying for the others.

Check Yourself

1. List specific responsibilities of the teacher during each of these activities:
    Bible Study
    Bible Sharing
    Bible Learning Activities
2. Evaluate your present effort as a teacher in relation to the duties you have just described.

3. Identify specific areas of your teaching ministry which need strengthening.

For Further Reading

Ways to Plan and Organize (chapter 5) provides an excellent summary of the role of the teacher.

Ways to Help Them Learn (chapter 5) discusses the importance of the teacher as a "Learning Enabler."

Bible Learning Activities (chapter 3) gives additional information concerning the teacher as facilitator.

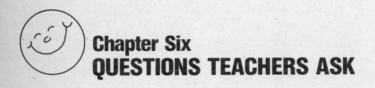

Chapter Six
QUESTIONS TEACHERS ASK

As a teacher, you probably have some other questions about your responsibilities. Here are a few questions teachers often ask . . .

How Can You Guide a Child
to Become a Member of God's Family?

One of the greatest privileges of serving as a Sunday School teacher is to help children learn how they can become members of God's family.

You will need to be aware of the background and maturity level of each child. Some children, especially from Christian homes, may be ready to believe in Jesus Christ as his Saviour earlier than others. Pray that the Holy Spirit will give you wisdom and keep you sensitive to every child's spiritual need. Remember, salvation is a supernatural work of the Holy Spirit and is the result of God Himself speaking to the child. Your role is to guide the child to discover how he can become a Christian.

Because children are easily influenced to follow the group, avoid group decisions. Plan opportunities to talk and pray individually with any child who desires to become a member of God's family.

Follow these basic steps in talking simply with the child about how to become a member of God's family. (The booklet, *God Wants YOU to Be a Member of His Family,* is an effective guide to follow as you talk and pray with each child. Show him what God says in His Word.)

1. God loves YOU very much. He wants you to become a member of His Family (1 John 4:8).

2. You and all the people in the world have done wrong things (Rom. 3:23). The Bible word for doing wrong is *sin.* God says you have sinned and sin must be punished (Rom. 6:23).

3. God loves you so much He sent His Son to die on the cross for your sin. Because Jesus never sinned, He is the only one who can take the punishment for your sin. (See Rom. 5:8; 2 Cor. 5:21; or 1 John 4:14.)

4. Are you sorry for your sin? Tell God now that you are. Do you believe Jesus loves you and died to be your Saviour? If you are sorry, and if you do believe in Jesus, God forgives all your sin. He makes everything all right between you and Him. (See John 1:12.)

5. The Bible says that when you believe in Jesus, God's Son, you receive God's gift of eternal life (John 3:16). This means God is with you now and forever.

As each child prays to receive Christ as his Saviour, allow him to express himself in his own way. His own prayer of faith should be meaningful to him.

Follow this prayer time with brief moments of conversation to clarify his decision. Remember to encourage, pray for him frequently, and provide for additional spiritual nurturing.

If you use the *God Wants YOU* booklet, student may sign it and keep it in his Bible as a record of his decision to believe in the Lord Jesus. Explain that he is to read the booklet again and again. It has the verses which you read together. The book tells him where to find other Bible verses which teach him what the Lord wants him to do now.

Other helpful booklets for new members of God's family are *God Wants YOU to Know How to Live as His Child; God Wants YOU to Talk to Him About Everything,* and *God Wants YOU to Know He Cares for You.* Have copies of these booklets available for your children.

Encourage the child to tell his parents about his decision if he wants to. Arrange to talk with his parents about the decision he has made. They may be interested in seeing a copy of the *God Wants You* booklet and the biblical steps in becoming a member of God's family you used in talking with their child. (Be alert to the Holy Spirit's working in the heart of a parent who may also be ready to become a child of God. Remember that your ministry with children includes their families as well.) Show parents the other helpful booklets in *God Wants You* series and suggest ways they can use these as a family to grow spiritually. Assure them that their interest and participation in their child's student book assignments each week will encourage his living and growing as a member of God's family.

How Do You Build Relationships with Your Students?

Your calling as a teacher of children involves you in a ministry to the whole child—with all of his physical, emotional, spiritual, social and intellectual needs. The importance of close relationships with each of your children becomes obvious if you are to gear Bible truths to specific needs children have.

What are some simple techniques which can be used to build close relationships with your children?

Get to Know Them

In one sense, you are a "detective" as you teach. Look for clues that will identify areas of interest and need for each child. Devising a simple chart can help you gear your teaching in this direction. Put the names of all of your children on a chart such as the one shown below, or have one page per child. Fill in pertinent

information as you become aware of it through observation and conversation: Does the child come from a happy home? Does he feel good about himself? What problems bother him? Consult with other members of your departmental team so that you have insights from several people who work with the child on Sundays.

NEEDS CHART

NEEDS	CHILD 1	CHILD 2	CHILD 3
SPIRITUAL What is his understanding of what it means to be a member of God's family?			
SOCIAL Shy? Aggressive? Need attention? Need more freedom? Need more structure?			
EDUCATIONAL Learn quickly? Learn slowly?			
SPECIAL INTERESTS Hobbies? Skills? Talents? Enjoys most?			
FAMILY BACKGROUND Father? Mother? Brothers and/or sisters?			
SPECIAL NEEDS Feel good about himself? Any problems that bother him?			

Let Each Child Know He Is Important to You

Here are some tips for helping each child in your class know that HE is an important and special person to you.

1. Use the child's name often in your conversation with him.

2. Commend each child at least once each Sunday for some good thing he has done. Be specific. "Jon, I really liked the way you kept working on your picture."

3. Give each child individual attention during each Sunday School session.

4. Use "active listening"—showing genuine interest in what the child says, rather than letting your mind wander or race ahead to what you are going to say next. Ask simple questions to encourage child to express himself, also to reflect the way he seems to feel. "Diane, I think you really like to ride your bike. What else do you like to do?" Restating what the child has said is an important aspect of active listening as well.

5. Smile often to let a child know you love and accept him "as is" and that you are glad he came.

6. Letter the caption "Notes for You" on one section of a bulletin board. Add personal notes such as "David: You did your very BEST work this morning," or "Karen: Thank you for putting things away so well last week." Add interest by lettering notes on different sizes, shapes and colors of paper. Print in large letters.

7. You can do extra things for a child that relate to his interests—like mailing him a baseball cartoon if he likes baseball; saving envelopes for him from your first-class mail if he collects stamps.

Be with Them During the Week

There is no general formula for showing a child you care. Rather, the Holy Spirit uses your personality and stewardship of time and abilities to spontaneously minister to children. You can minister by what you say and do all week long with a child. He talks about and remembers all the extras.

1. Visit Him

Busy people, how can you make all the extra contacts that build relationships?

Here is an idea. Mark on a map all the residences of the children in your class or department. Keep the map in your car and survey it as you set out on errands during the year. Drive by a home and stop for just a minute to express your interest in whatever the child's doing. Leave a note for *him,* if he's not at home.

2. Get in on the Big Events in a Child's Life

Encourage the children to let you know if something special for them will happen—a musical recital, sports event, school program, birthday party. When you come to a big event, you learn more about the child and also show him you care. Afterwards mail him a note congratulating him for his performance and thanking him for the invitation.

3. Take Him Along with You

Call ahead and ask the parents if you can include a child in your plans. Perhaps you need to run some errands—grocery shopping or shopping for Sunday School supplies. Use time traveling in the car to get to know the child. He will feel honored just to "run around" with you. Get a hamburger or something else the child especially enjoys.

Teach children to serve the Lord by taking them to serve others. Take them with you to visit someone who is sick or elderly. Take a friendly child with you to visit a student who has not been attending Sunday School regularly. (You may find yourself chatting with a parent while the two children go off to play.)

As weather permits, take children into the outdoors. Have a progressive park party—eat sandwiches at the first park, fruit at another and ice cream at the last. Use outdoors experiences to enlarge each child's understanding of the greatness of God.

4. Take a Child Home with You

He wonders what you are really like. Where do you live? What is your family like? What is your job? Do you have hobbies? What sad and funny things happen to you? What are you like as a Christian when you're home?

Invite a child to your home and you won't remain a stranger

to him. The more comfortable he is with you, the better you can minister to him. You may be able to plan a schedule so you can invite one or two students to your home for Sunday lunch.

May the Lord grant you insights into children, and creative and sensitive means to minister to children! Offer your friendship for His sake!

How Can You Provide for Differences in Your Students' Abilities?

Reading Abilities

As in any school classroom you can expect a wide range of reading abilities even at one grade level. However, you will need to be even more alert to this if you find it necessary to combine two or more grades.

A quick way to appraise the reading ability of young children is to ask them to draw a line under all the words they know in a sentence in the Student's Guide; then, informally, listen to each child read the words he underlined. When you have a general impression of the reading level of each child, you can plan carefully how to adapt the use of materials that require reading.

Here are some ways you can help nonreaders or slower readers: (1) Read or tape information (from the Bible, Student's Guide, children's books, Teaching Resources cards, etc.) and let children listen to find answers to specific questions. (2) Let slow readers learn in other ways than reading (e.g., looking for information in pictures). Don't forget to praise slow readers just as warmly as rapid readers for information they share. (3) Let partners of varying abilities work together.

Writing Abilities

Remember that it takes a long time for young children to write— don't rush them! Some children can write more easily than others. Praise all children for the good work they do—not for the length of what they write.

Here are some ways you can work with children who don't enjoy writing or who are just learning to write: (1) Let them draw a picture and write a few words to go with the picture. (2) Let them dictate a sentence or story to the teacher or an assistant who letters or types it as it is dictated. (3) Let children dictate their sentences, stories or Bible verses on tape, to be played when their activity is shared with the large group. (4) Let a group of children dictate a story, each contributing some part of the story; teacher letters story on chart or in a booklet for children to illustrate. (5) Provide children with "story-starters"—let them write endings to unfinished sentences or stories, rather than writing an entire story. (6) Let children who do not enjoy writing do some other part of a project, as illustrating a Bible verse or a story the group is working on.

How Can You Help Children Get Started with Bible Readiness Choices as Soon as They Arrive?

Establish a pattern so the students in your class know they are to come to your teaching area as soon as they arrive, and that they are to begin to work immediately—even though you may be helping another child.

Place an assignment chart in the same location each Sunday so children can go immediately to their chart to see what to do. You can: (1) use sentence strips in a pocket chart as shown in lesson sketches; or (2) pin sentence strips to a bulletin board; or (3) letter instructions on a chalkboard or chart. If the reading skills of your learners are limited, use simple drawings, pictures or sample pages to make the directions clear.

Be sure all materials are easily accessible to children (e.g., on a nearby table or shelf). To make it possible for children to work more independently, you may wish to place the materials for a particular choice near a stand-up card that tells how to use the materials.

For variety, or for slower readers, you might put some instructions on a cassette tape.

When you provide more than one choice, at least one of them should require a minimum of teacher help so there will always be something the learner can do by himself when you are working with another child.

How Can You Motivate Children to Memorize Bible Verses?

The easiest and most effective way to memorize God's Word is to use it with understanding in a variety of meaningful Bible learning experiences. As often as possible, use Bible verses in your conversation and discussion. From time to time, ask questions that children can answer with the Bible Verse to Know, as "What Bible verse tells you what you should do when your parents tell you to do something?" Or, "What is the main idea in this verse?" To make sure children understand the meaning of a verse, let them say it in their own words or tell how they can do what it says.

Use Bible Learning Games* that help children memorize Bible verses with understanding.

Recognize individual differences; encourage each child to do his

---

*Suggested in your G/L Teacher's Manual or in the Teaching Resources.

best work, and praise him for it. Give extra time to children who do not receive help at home.

How Can You Guide Students in Use of Student Guide?

The Student Guide is a valuable teaching/learning tool. These pages can be a good indication of what takes root in a child's mind and heart by giving him opportunity to express what he is learning. The following ideas will help you use the Guide effectively.

What's on the Pages of the Guide?

Materials for each lesson involve students at Sunday School as well as provide home activities. Variety and colorful appearance are keys to motivating and maintaining interest in Bible learning.

Activities to be completed in class reinforce the Bible study and help students (1) learn important background information for understanding the Bible story; (2) learn and use new Bible words; (3) read Bible stories and verses; (4) understand and apply Bible verses; and (5) plan ways to do what God's Word says. Students work on these activities individually and in groups.

Home Bible study assignments include putting into action specific plans made in class; Bible verses to think about and obey; projects to help apply Scripture to daily experiences.

Additional resources (such as maps and time lines) will be used during Bible study throughout each course for older children.

What Motivates Students to Complete
Guide Assignments at Home?

1. *As you assign and explain work to be done at home,* ask, "Is there anything that looks hard for you to finish?" Answer any questions they may have about the assignments.

2. *Help students think of ideas and begin* doing the Guide sheet during class to create an interest in continuing at home. Sharing ideas in class helps children decide what to do. Slow and hard-to-motivate students are often encouraged when they hear others are interested and when they themselves help suggest ideas.

3. *When a child comes to class without his Guide sheet,* don't make

an issue of it. Suggest he bring the completed work next week. Ask, "What is a good time for you to work on your study?" Make a note, and call during the week to encourage him. This encourages success instead of expecting failure.

4. *For absentees,* mail Guide sheets with note telling child he was missed and encouraging him to complete the work.

5. *Enlist parents' cooperation* in person. Suggest they work with their child and by assuring them you are willing to help.

6. *If a student is having trouble completing assignments,* call parents and suggest working together to adjust assignments or give alternate ones to encourage and help him.

Check Yourself

1. Discuss ways to build relationships with the children in your class, both on Sunday morning and during the week.

2. Share at regular planning meetings with other staff members successful ways you have built close relationships with your children.

3. List at least three ways to provide for differences in ability among your children (especially in reading and writing skills).

4. Using *God Wants YOU to Be a Member of His Family* booklet, role-play with another staff member at staff meeting how to guide a child to become a Christian.

5. Discuss the importance of memory work and the use of the Student Guide. How can these aspects of your Sunday School program be strengthened?

For Further Reading

Ways to Help Them Learn (chapter 5) has many helpful hints on the questions just discussed.

Bible Learning Activities (chapter 6) includes helpful hints on how to build effective relationships with children.

Ways to Help Them Learn (chapters 1–3) describes needs and patterns of growth of various age levels of children.

Bible Learning Activities (chapter 2) gives additional help on the needs of children.

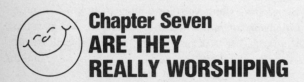

Chapter Seven
ARE THEY
REALLY WORSHIPING

"I want to help children learn to worship," you say. Yet when they sit tall, silent, hands folded and sing on cue, you still may wonder, "Are they really worshiping?" Here are some pointers to help you decide.

What Is Worship Anyway?

Worship is a spontaneous or a gradual response to an awareness of God's presence, wisdom, power, love. It may be an attitude, a feeling, an expression of gratitude, wonder, love, excitement or praise. Worship may take the form of a prayer, a gift, a song or even silent awe at the wonder of God. It may be verbal, or nonverbal; a facial expression, a smile, a tear, a look of surprise. Perhaps it will come simply in words like "WOW!" or "God sure is important!"

Whatever form worship takes, it includes recognition that God is present, all-wise, powerful and loving. And it will involve a response to that awareness.

When Do Students Worship?

Worship can occur anytime—during Bible Study, Bible Learning Activities, Sharing time, or at home, during the week, inside, outside, *anywhere* and *anytime*. Likewise, worship may not occur at times we plan it, and it will not always occur for two students at the same time. It's an individual response arising from within each student.

How Do You Help Students Worship?

1. *Be sensitive* to the needs and attitudes of children. Encourage them to express their feelings; lead them to discover God's greatness; pray about the things they share; and show genuine concern and interest, no matter how small the discovery is which they are making about God.

2. *Be an example.* Henrietta Mears said, "You teach a little by what you say. You teach most by what you are." Children learn and copy the attitudes of adults around them. Begin by developing your own attitudes of worship. Remind yourself of the Lord's presence and love for you. Let the children see your love for the Lord and how you express it. Your tone of voice, attitudes and small comments will set the mood.

Pray simply, directly and naturally—like talking to a friend. Pray about a variety of things and at spontaneous times so that students will learn that prayer is appropriate at any time.

3. *Provide natural, comfortable opportunities* for children to worship. Don't insist children worship, but lead them into experiences. For example, if students are sharing problems, pause briefly to ask God's guidance. If you are speaking of blessings, let each child say a sentence thank-you prayer.

Help children discover things they can thank God for, gifts they can give to God, ways they can serve God, moments when God is especially near, and other experiences that bring worship as a response. For example, one teacher on a weekend retreat was sitting on a mountain with her students when the stars came out. In the silence as the first star appeared, she casually commented, "Have you ever counted all the stars? The Bible says God knows exactly how many stars there are." After a brief silence, one boy spoke up, "You mean He knows *exactly* how many? All those stars?" "Yes."

43

"WOW!" A word of praise from the heart of a child as he realized God's majesty and greatness.

Not all children worship at the same time. You cannot make children worship. But you can help them become aware of God's presence; teach them ways to respond; and provide opportunities to do so.

Give your children opportunities to worship by playing musical instruments. Toy stores have inexpensive musical instruments that can be played even by children who have no musical background (e.g., bells, zither, toy organs with color-coded keys).

In singing, don't "just fill up time." Use songs that build on what students are studying. Such comments as, "Let's sing about what a joy it is to have Jesus as a friend and how He will help us," can turn singing a song into an opportunity to express thankfulness and love to God.

Children who hesitate to participate and share in other ways will often be motivated to express their worship and praise through music. And their successful feeling in this area will sometimes encourage them to participate in other ways.

Check Yourself

1. Define worship. Why is guiding children in moments of worship an important part of your Sunday School ministry?

2. List three helpful hints for guiding children in worship.

3. Evaluate your present use of worship time in Sunday School. How can you improve opportunities for children to worship?

For Further Reading

Ways to Help Them Learn (chapter 13) provides excellent resources for strengthening the music and worship program through your Sunday School.

Chapter Eight
DISCIPLINE WITH LOVE

Bernice Hilton stopped in the Sunday School office one Sunday and exclaimed, "I've had it!" Those children are absolutely impossible! I spend most of my time telling them to be quiet and listen to me. By the time the children are settled down, I have only a few minutes to lead the Bible Study. I've tried everything—from bribing them with candy to pleading with them—and Billy Jones keeps right on disrupting our class. What can I do?"

As a teacher or leader of children in Sunday School, you may have reached this point of exasperation with your group. How do you handle children who spend more time disrupting your class than cooperating?

Let's define what discipline is, and then list several important guidelines to help children enjoy studying God's Word together.

What Is Discipline Anyway?

Some people immediately think of strict rules to obey or some kind of punishment when they think of discipline. Actually, discipline

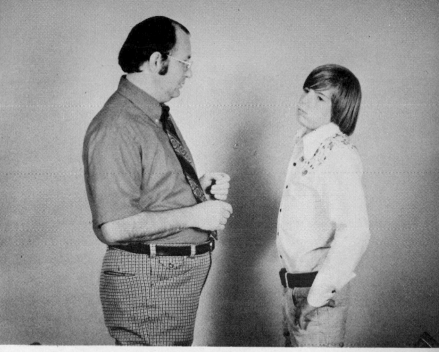

is *not* what you do to a child. Rather, it is what you do with and for the child to indicate that you value him as an individual and want to strengthen his desires to be and to do his best.

This should be the thrust of whatever discipline is needed in the Sunday School—that it serve to strengthen rather than to discourage children.

Perhaps you're asking how this positive approach to discipline is possible, especially with the limited amount of time you have available on a Sunday morning. Here are several specific suggestions to guide you.

Respect Your Children

Basic to effective teaching is an attitude of respect and acceptance for each child. Your attitude will set the mood for your class—a mood the children will reflect. If you trust your children, they generally will trust you. If your attitude is condescending or non-accepting, your children will respond with a similar attitude toward you. If you yourself are eager to learn, concerned about the needs of your children, and happy to be with the group, your children will soon be reflecting similar feelings.

Be Positive

God's Word reminds us, "A pleasant teacher is the best" (Prov. 16:21). Are you pleasant to be with? Are you genuine in your love for children?

The words you say and your tone of voice often determine the ways children respond. So, to guide children effectively, you will want to use phrases that help you get the point across without alienating the child. For instance, say, "What we start we need to finish", instead of, "You have to finish your work." Other key phrases are "Please help us by . . ." "We need you to . . ." "You need to . . ." and "You may . . ." For example, when you ask, "Which activity do you want to do?" a child may reply, "None of them!" Answer him, "You may (or we need you to) do this activity." Help him know you expect him to make choices.

Don't spend time worrying about the times you do not communicate effectively or provide the proper setting for your class. Learn from your mistakes. Rejoice when you succeed. Learn from the effective techniques of others teaching with you.

Know Your Children

As in every generation, children bring their own needs and problems with them to Sunday School. The causes and implications are legion. Some children are passive and cooperative, while others come with a "let's-see-what-we-can-get-by-with" attitude.

As soon as possible, identify the needs of your children. What kinds of homes do they come from? Do you know the parents? How is each child doing in school? Does he make friends easily? What is the child's attitude toward authority? What is his relationship to God? Keep a notebook with a section for each child. Jot down observations each week. Pray for the children by name as you prepare for each session. (See chapter 6 for ideas on how to build relationships with your children.)

Some children need attention so desperately that they will go to any length to get it. Ignoring discipline problems does not help, but neither does giving a great deal of precious class time to commanding a child to behave. Getting to know your children during the week will help prevent serious disruptions in class.

Be Organized

Children learn best in an atmosphere which provides some measure of order and purpose the learner understands. A confused, disorganized atmosphere rarely allows for meaningful learning.

Discipline problems often arise when the children sense the teacher is not prepared. Lavish your effort and time on preparation for Sunday. Then you can lavish interest and time on your children Sunday morning.

From the moment children begin arriving, they are ready for learning activities. Plan for early arrival time by having your room ready for instant use! Invest your time then in giving attention to each child as he arrives.

Plan your sessions with sufficient variety so that the children are not expected to be inactive for more than a few minutes at a time. Children have a great deal of energy you can channel into learning that will be fun and interesting.

As you plan for the best use of your Sunday School period, keep the individual needs of your children in mind. Capitalize on their gifts and abilities. Some very energetic children will need a more active Bible learning experience than children who are more quiet and shy. So, provide for more than one type of learning activity.

Involve Children

Be sure that each activity has purpose and is obviously related to the aim of the lesson. Children are quick to sense the difference between "busy work" and activity with purpose.

From the beginning, involve the children in the class experience by delegating responsibilities, such as setting up equipment, reading Scripture, handing out papers and supplies, writing on the chalkboard, and even presenting portions of the lesson. Phrases such as "Nice going," "Good for you," and "Keep up the good work" should become important phrases in the vocabulary of every leader of children.

Evaluate

After each Sunday School session recall the situations that may have caused discipline problems. If, for example, all groups go to Bible learning activities at the same moment and this causes pandemonium, allow only one group to be dismissed at a time, giving each specific directions to follow when they get there.

Keep the activities moving. A slow pace causes boredom. Boredom increases discipline problems. The teachers need to cooperate by bringing the classes promptly to the large group when the signal is given so the others will not have to wait.

Set and Enforce Realistic Standards

Children will obey standards which are realistic and often are well able to contribute ideas for these standards.

If you insist, for example, that there be no talking during Bible learning activities, you set an unrealistic standard that will produce tension in the group. Soon several of the group will divert their attention from your carefully planned activity and you will find yourself spending more time enforcing silence than helping your students learn.

Should you keep silent, then, and let the children talk? No! Set a realistic standard. You should say, "It is important that we pay close attention to our Bible learning activity. Let's talk about what we are doing." An atmosphere of informality and trust will enhance your learning experience.

Children do not respect or obey the teacher who does not enforce his own rules. When you set a standard, make a mental or written note of it. You may say, "We need to clean up our table before we leave today," then find yourself doing the cleanup. Next time write this standard on a chalkboard or ask several children to remind you.

Minimize the time and attention you spend correcting children. Remember that their misconduct is not a federal offense. Be quick to forgive. What correcting you must do should be done as privately as possible. To shame a child publicly before others can only have bad results: to give a child the attention he couldn't get by positive means—even though it be negative; or, to depreciate before others the worth of a person whom God dearly loves.

You help a child respect authority as you consistently enforce realistic standards. Helping a child to obey is an important step in helping him choose to respect and to obey God. Be sure the child understands why these rules are important to the group as well as to you. Patiently and firmly insist on your standards. The child needs this security of knowing you are consistent. Help him know that you are in charge and that he can trust you to be fair.

Ask Other Staff Members for Help

Seek to deal with the child's need for help. But if your attempts do not succeed, alert your department leader before another Sunday goes by. You are not failing by asking for help. Rather, you are failing if you do not recognize your need for help and do not ask for it.

Involve other members of your department team to give you information and insights as they observe you with children. Make children with special needs a matter for prayer and discussion in your staff meetings.

Communicate with Parents

Keep in close touch with the parents of your children during the year. Plan several informal contacts with the parents, both on an individual family basis, and with families of the entire group. Picnics, hikes, parties and other informal get-togethers can do wonders for developing rapport among your families. Keep families informed about what your class is doing. Establish a support system in which you let the parents know that you are willing to help them in whatever ways you can.

A relationship of rapport will provide you with a natural channel for communication if a special problem arises. Seek their counsel by explaining the problem briefly and then asking for their help.

Above All, Love

God's Word tells us, "Most important of all, continue to show deep love for each other, for love makes up for many of your faults" (1 Pet. 4:8, *TLB*). Remember, God's love for you does not depend on your good behavior! Don't allow your love for the children to depend on their good behavior! Love them as they are, and resolve to be the kind of leader Christ intended you to be—a wise teacher who makes learning a joy.

Check Yourself

1. Define the word "discipline" in your own words. Compare your definition with that provided at the beginning of this chapter.

2. List several specific guidelines necessary for making Bible Study a happy experience for your children. Make suggestions on how each of these guidelines can be implemented in your Sunday School.

3. Share recent situations you have experienced where you have dealt (whether successfully or unsuccessfully) with specific needs of your children.

4. How are you involving parents in your Sunday School program with children? Plan ways to strengthen church/home ties.

For Further Reading

Bible Learning Activities (chapter 6) provides excellent resources for dealing with behavior challenges.

Chapter Nine
ROOM ENVIRONMENT AND SUPPLIES

As a child enters your Sunday School department, he should feel, "This is a good place to be. I like it here."

Room appearance—its arrangement, color, cleanliness—makes a definite impression on children and their parents. Hopefully, your room communicates openness and excitement. A poorly arranged, untidy room decorated in drab colors can communicate disinterest, dullness and boredom. Surely there is no greater mistake than creating an atmosphere that allows boredom as a response to the teaching of God's Word.

Begin by asking yourself how you can make better use of the area you have. Are there doors which may be taken off small adjoining rooms? Some partitions which may be removed to allow more open space? Any excess furniture (tables not used, broken chairs, storage boxes) you could remove? Is there an unused closet or bookcase in the room which could be converted into an interest center or supply corner?

Work as a staff to plan the best and most attractive use of facilities and space available to you.

Present your needs to members of your church boards and listen to their suggestions. Think big and attempt to use the facilities you have to the very best advantage and to the glory of God!

What Are Some of the Basic Supplies
You Should Have on Hand for Bible Learning Activities?

For most of the Bible learning activities you will need supplies such as: pencils; paper in various sizes, colors and weights; crayons or felt pens; scissors; paste; shelf paper or newsprint. (Newsprint is usually available for a nominal cost from local newspaper offices.) A pencil sharpener in the room is helpful. Check the Teacher's Manual for special materials which may occasionally be needed—scraps of fabric, lightweight wire, Play-Doh, etc.

Have a supply of pictures on hand for use in collages, montages, decoupages and other projects. Collect pictures from magazines, greeting cards, old Sunday School books, Sunday bulletins and other sources. Make a file—or simply use a large box for storing pictures. Don't worry about trimming the pictures . . . students can do that later.

Colorfully decorated coffee cans and boxes make good containers for collecting such miscellaneous items as spools, yarn scraps, rubber bands, wheels from broken toys, small bottles, artificial flowers, etc.

If time is limited, you may wish to have supplies available at work area ahead of time.

How Can You Have Activities Which Use Paint or Paste
When Your Room Is not Near a Washroom or Water?

Use plastic buckets or large coffee cans and bring water into the room—one bucket for clean water, the other for dirty water. The department leader, a teacher, or some of the older children may be responsible for bringing water into the room when needed. Use small sponges to clean tabletops. Have plenty of paper towels and a box of cleansing tissues on hand. Empty water at end of session.

Who Is Responsible for Cleanup?

Students will quickly learn good stewardship when they learn they are responsible for putting all supplies into their proper places, picking up wastepaper and other scraps from floor, and leaving their department room generally neat. Cheerful adult supervision will soon make students realize that "cleanup" is *always* part of an activity!

How Should We Store Supplies?

Keep supplies in a central cabinet, closet, table or bookshelf in the department room so students designated may easily get supplies. Someone may need to be in the supply area when students pick up supplies for their own groups, to help them find what they need and encourage them to return promptly to their groups. If time is limited, have supplies available at work areas ahead of time.

Supplies properly stored save money and lead to greater efficiency. *Charts* may be preserved by clipping them on women's skirt hangers and hanging them on the wall of a closet. *Glue bottles* will be ready to be carried to various tables in the room if they are stored in soft-drink cartons. Paint or cover cartons with adhesive paper. Cartons hold six to eight bottles of glue each. *Tempera paint* which has been stored in translucent detergent bottles is much easier to handle. Shake bottle (to stir paint) before use. Add liquid detergent (1 tbs./qt.) to paint. This helps in cleaning brushes and prevents cracking when paint dries on murals. *Scissors* may be stored in numerous ways. Punch openings in the lid of a plastic egg carton or the plastic lid of a coffee can. Or punch holes in vertical rows (6 holes per row) in a one-gallon plastic bleach bottle.

Check Yourself

1. Why is room appearance and organization of materials important in your Sunday School?

2. Evaluate your present use of space. What do you think your Sunday School department says to a child who enters it? What improvements need to be made?

3. How are your supplies stored? Any need to organize your supplies more efficiently? What supplies should be ordered to better meet your Sunday-by-Sunday needs?

4. List any equipment/supply needs which need to be shared with your church board. Plan to submit your list as soon as possible.

For Further Reading

Ways to Plan and Organize has an excellent chapter (6) on the importance of your facilities. The charts on room arrangements are especially helpful.

Ways to Help Them Learn provides additional guidance (chapter 6) on this subject.

Bible Learning Activities gives a list of basic supplies needed for creative teaching (pp. 57,58).

Chapter Ten
SPECIAL EMPHASES
IN THE SUNDAY SCHOOL YEAR

Throughout the Sunday School year, you will probably have several special emphases, including Promotion Sunday, seasonal programs, missions and special service projects. Here are some hints on how to make these experiences exciting and how to guide them efficiently.

Promotion Sunday

Children need to have a warm, happy, unhurried experience their first Sunday in a new department. Here are some ideas to consider:

1. Time, waiting and confusion can be saved if all children who are to be promoted—from all departments—move at the same time. You can use a signal such as a bell.

2. Use name tags for the first few Sundays so you can call each student by name.

3. Here's a simple way to move children from one department to another and help them know immediately who their new teacher is: Before Promotion Sunday, make a name tag for each child and each teacher, using a different color for each class. Before Sunday School, give the children's name tags to the department leader or secretary of the department *from* which the children will be promoted. This person pins the name tags on the children as they arrive. At whatever time the children are to be promoted, the new department leader goes to their department, greets them and leads them to their new department. In the new department the children meet in their

large department group for 10 to 15 minutes and then divide into class groups according to the color of their name tags. Each child can immediately see who his teacher is when teachers are introduced, because each teacher is wearing the same color name tag his class is wearing.

A Schedule for Promotion Sunday

Your main purpose on Promotion Sunday is to get to know your new students, help them feel comfortable and happy in their new surroundings, and motivate interest in the Bible study they will be doing during the coming year. Here is a schedule that will help you accomplish this; adapt it to meet your needs.

Moving to new department: 15–20 minutes

This includes arrival and meeting in previous department and moving to new department.

Department group: 10–15 minutes

Greet new children and let them know how glad you are to have them in your department. Let them sing for you a song they enjoyed in their other department.

Tell what children need to know about procedures and their new room: where to hang coats, where supplies are. Introduce department staff. Give simple directions and dismiss one class at a time, with its new teacher. Reinforce good behavior, e.g., comment on how well classes leave.

Small permanent class groups: 30–35 minutes

Get acquainted with children by playing this simple game to learn names: After a few moments' study, children cover name tags with their hands and see if you can say their names correctly. Then let children take turns seeing if they can say all the names (including yours) correctly.

Ask each child in your group to draw the following on a sheet of paper: pictures of all the people in their families, their pets, friends, homes, any favorite activities, etc. Put completed sheets on a bulletin board with caption, "All About Us." You may want to ask someone to take a picture of you and your class to add to the bulletin board.

Explain class procedures. Tell children to come directly to your class area when they arrive next Sunday. Show them one of the activities they will work on next Sunday. Create interest and enthusiasm for the exciting Bible learning activities they will work on as they study God's Word together.

Discuss how to work well together. List these points: (1) Be polite. (2) Safety first. (3) Take care of property—yours and others. (4) Be a learner. Don't bother others.

Then ask questions to guide children to set up a few specific procedures. For example, point to "Be polite." Say, "Suppose several people want to say something at the same time. What signal can you give to show you have something to say?" Children will probably suggest raising hands. "Suppose you are making something and two people want the glue at the same time. What can you do?"

Keep list short. You can add to it later as needed.

Today, and in future class sessions, look for ways of reinforcing good behavior. For example, "I'm glad to see how you (gave Terry first choice)."

This first session with your students can be an important key to a successful year. Use it to get acquainted, to let each child know he is important to you, to set up a few simple rules for working together, to motivate interest in the Bible Study for the coming year.

Planning Your Year

Since there are fifty-two Bible lessons given for the year, consider omitting one lesson or combining two lessons at some point in the year. This will make it possible to use Promotion Sunday to get acquainted with new children and to set up procedures that will enable you to do a better job of teaching throughout the year.

Following up on Absentees

The teacher or secretary should visit, telephone or write to each absentee. Here's a sample letter: "We missed you, Karen. When you come to Sunday School next Sunday, you and the rest of your class will be in a new department. We meet in Room 10. Your new teacher is Mr. Lee."

Incidentally, each teacher should occasionally also telephone or write each student who was present to let the child know that he is appreciated in some special way.

Seasonal Emphases

Throughout the year, you may want to highlight seasonal emphases, such as Christmas and Easter, which have particular importance for Christians everywhere. Your curriculum should provide special lessons or units which will guide you to make these seasons memorable for your children.

Remember the following as you plan:
• Plan your calendar so that Christmas and Easter celebrations fall on the appropriate Sundays. Expand to a unit-long seasonal study if possible.
• Consider a modified schedule which will allow for these special emphases. Have you ever invited parents for a Christmas or Easter Sunday?
• Plan special decorations to add to the festive spirit of the holiday you are celebrating.
• Send invitations to everyone so that they are informed of your plans.
• Be sure the children understand the Christian meaning of these holidays.
• Provide simple refreshments at the conclusion of the hour.

Missions Projects

"God, please bless the missionaries!" some Sunday School children dutifully pray.

Teachers, this general prayer is all you can expect them to pray UNLESS you give the children in your Sunday School a specific need to pray about, or a specific project to which they can give money or time. Here are several specific projects your department can consider for a focus on world mission. These opportunities can only motivate your students to be interested in missions if you begin to make them happen a MONTH OR TWO IN ADVANCE! Focus on the unique ministries of your church or denomination as you prepare.

Get addresses of missionaries the children can write to. Choose missionaries in various occupations. Select one field or various locations.

Write ahead to these missionaries. Say, for example, "In four or five weeks children in our Sunday School department will write you letters. Our study of missions to a large part depends on your cooperation. All we need is a quick postcard letting us know (1) what specific things we can pray about; and (2) what project or small gift of money we can share with you. These children will be most anxious to receive your answer. You may wish to address one postcard to several children." This is a good time to mail these missionaries money to spend for postcards, pictures and curios you may like them to mail back to you.

Research prayer needs of missionaries. You will need to know specific prayer requests even before the missionaries write back. Pool information from staff and church members. List needs each missionary may have—money, supplies, friends, schools for children. Does he need prayer for learning a new language? Prayer for more believers in his area? Prayer that the believers grow in their faith? Research these needs and children can begin to pray specifically and thank God for specific answers!

Plan a project to involve the children in giving their time, money or possessions. Contact your church missions committee or denominational office for information. If you need a source of information or don't have denomination headquarters, you may write to the publishers of these materials for sources of information. Or, the idea for your project may come directly from your correspondence with the missionaries. You may choose to make puppets; collect greeting cards, food, clothing, toys, books; cut out magazine pictures or pictures from old Sunday School materials. Your students will be thrilled to have such a special role.

Make a tabletop display for your project as in sketch. Let the children suggest what they can do without, such as ice cream, candy, toys, part of their allowance. Use a glass jar to collect the visible results.

After you have secured addresses of missionaries, written to let them know what to expect, compiled a list of specific prayer requests and planned a project, you may wish to choose from the following, ideas to enhance the children's understanding and involvement in missions.

1. Schedule a *visitor* to tell a true mission story. Your guest may be a missionary or one who has visited a mission field. Use high school or college students who have been on short-term mission assignments. Before the guest arrives, have the children write questions to ask. Later they can make a written or oral report on what they have learned.

2. Have a *tape exchange.* Make a tape to mail to your missionaries. Include songs and verses from the group, news about your Sunday School activities, and questions the children want to ask.

Let the children do the asking. "Hello! My name is Bill. I would like to know if . . . ?" This way the missionary will be able to answer Bill (and the group) specifically.

Also, record the children praying for missions (more effective if they do not know their prayers are being recorded). The prayers of the children will encourage the missionaries.

Leave room at the end of the tape for missionaries to reply with songs, news and answers to questions. Send postage money for return of tape.

3. Make a *display* for others in your church to see. Supply the

missionaries money to send curios you can display. Have the children do the planning for the display. The ideas behind the display will remain with them longer if they have had a part in the planning.

4. Make a chart listing *the birthdays of missionaries and their children.* Make cards for upcoming birthdays.

5. Listen to a *record in another language and learn a song* in another language.

6. Have a *picture exchange.* Have duplicates made of pictures of missionaries so each child in department can use it to make a prayer reminder. Send pictures of your children or department to mission field so they can also have prayer reminders for you.

7. Preview a *missions film,* if available.

8. *Listening post* (record a missionary story on cassette tape for children to hear with earphones).

Service Projects

As a department, you also need to see needs and opportunities for service close to home. The curriculum for children provides several units with service project possibilities suggested.

Here are a few ideas for you to consider for your Sunday School or church-time ministry:

● Do a project for some other group in the church—such as sanding blocks for preschoolers, providing a musical program or worship service for an adult class.

● Inquire about any work which needs to be done on your church grounds, such as cleanup, weeding, etc.

● Find a special need in your community which you as a group can meet. Check with local civic or community centers, YMCA or other service organization which might appreciate your assistance.

● Invite children from another church to join your children for a picnic or party. Plan get-acquainted games and other means for the children to enjoy each other's company.

● Plan group visit to a place with a special ministry, such as an inner-city church, rescue mission or convalescent home. Consult with leaders of these groups to find ways to follow up your visit with on ongoing project.

As a group, select the project which seems to be most meaningful and fits within the boundaries of your schedule, resources, etc.

These projects could be completed as part of a unit which focuses on the need to serve others, or as an ongoing project throughout the year. You will discover that your relationships with your children will deepen as you have a mutual project which reaches out to the needs of others. Guiding children to a deeper understanding of love for others is one of the greatest privileges of being a teacher or leader of children.

Check Yourself

1. Evaluate your procedures and practices for Promotion Sunday. Any need for better planning?

2. What are you doing concerning seasonal emphases (especially Christmas and Easter)? What plans need to be made to make these special seasons meaningful to the children in your Sunday School?

3. Brainstorm missions and/or service projects you as a department could do. Make specific plans for implementing these projects in the near future.

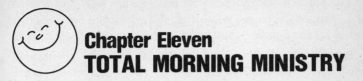

Chapter Eleven
TOTAL MORNING MINISTRY

Some churches have expanded their Sunday School hour to a total morning ministry of 2½ hours. There are several ways to adapt

PLAN I For Sunday School and Churchtime

Activity	Group Size	Minutes
Building Bible Readiness	Small, permanent group	15
Exploring God's Word	Small, permanent group	20
Bible Sharing (Worship/ Special Emphasis)	Large group	20
Break (Refreshments/ Recreation)	Large group	15
Assemble for Worship	Large group	10
Participation in Church Service	Large group	20–25
Bible Learning Activities	Elective small groups	20–25
Praise Time (Singing/ Sharing/Praying)	Large group	10–15

Sunday School curriculum so that it will provide enough resources for the total morning.

Here are two basic plans many churches follow. The first plan includes participation in the adult worship service, while the other plan does not.

Many churches in a total morning session report that there is ample material in G/L curriculum for a 90-minute session. They use the remaining time for in-depth studies in worship, missions, music, memory work and service projects. They often recruit people with special interests to teach for a specified time. For example,

PLAN II for Sunday School and Churchtime

Activity	Group Size	Minutes
Building Bible Readiness	Small, permanent group	15
Exploring God's Word	Small, permanent group	20
Bible Sharing	Large group	20
Break (Refreshments/ Recreation)	Large group	15–20
Bible Learning Activities such as: Bible Learning games Science Drama Listening Post Creative Expression Art Writing Bible Learning Activities included in G/L curriculum.	Elective small groups (either 2 30-minute segments or a 45-minute segment followed by a 15-minute Informal Praise Time)	60

someone with musical ability might work with the children for several weeks on a choir number for Sunday School, church, or a convalescent home. Someone with an interest in missions might guide the children in a special study of the work of one of your missionaries, including a missions project. Someone interested in memory work can plan Bible verse games/activities.

Check Yourself

1. Discuss and evaluate the two plans suggested in this chapter. Does either plan meet the needs of your situation? Why or why not?

2. What needs to be done to expand your Sunday School program to a total morning ministry?

For Further Reading

For additional suggestions for how to plan a total morning ministry, see Chapter 7 of *Bible Learning Activities*.

 **Chapter Twelve**
WHERE CAN YOU GO FOR MORE HELP?

ICL Seminars

The International Center for Learning (ICL), a division of G/L Publications, provides a comprehensive training experience for thousands of teachers and leaders for ministry in Christian education in numerous cities. The three-day, age-level training experiences cover such subjects as age-level characteristics and needs, curriculum planning, creative Bible learning activities, planning the Sunday School hour, setting goals, and much more. Attending such a seminar with your staff will greatly enhance your effectiveness as a team of those ministering to children. Write International Center for Learning, 110 W. Broadway, Glendale, California 91204, for details.

Other Learning Opportunities

Look for other opportunities to develop skills as a teacher or leader. Denominational conferences, Sunday School association workshops, public school open houses, and observation at Sunday Schools which have developed effective programs are among the learning experiences from which you can profit.

ICL Insight Books

Most chapters in this book have referred to chapters in three books that are especially helpful on these topics:

Ways to Plan and Organize Your Sunday School: Children, Grades 1 to 6, by Charles T. Smith. Glendale, California: Regal Books, 1971.

Ways to Help Them Learn: Children, Grades 1 to 6, by Barbara J. Bolton. Glendale, California: Regal Books, 1972.

Bible Learning Activities: Children, Grades 1 to 6, by Barbara J. Bolton and Charles T. Smith. Glendale, California: Regal Books, 1973.

More Books

Here are a few additional books you will enjoy as you minister to children:

68283

Alexander, David S. *The New Testament in Living Pictures.* Glendale, California: Regal Books, 1972.

_____. *The Old Testament in Living Pictures.* Glendale, California: Regal Books, 1973.

Allstrom, Elizabeth. *You Can Teach Creatively.* Nashville: Abingdon Press, 1970.

Beers, V. Gilbert. *Learning to Read from the Bible Series:*
God Is My Helper
God Is My Friend
Jesus Is My Teacher
Jesus Is My Guide. Grand Rapids, Michigan: Zondervan Publishing House, 1973.

Briggs, Dorothy Corkille. *Your Child's Self-Esteem.* New York: Doubleday, 1970.

Brown, Lowell E., with Bobbie Reed. *Your Sunday School Can Grow.* Glendale, California: Regal Books, 1974.

Chamberlain, Eugene. *When Can a Child Really Believe?* Nashville: Broadman Press, 1973.

Dobson, James. *Dare to Discipline.* Glendale, California: Regal Books, 1970.

_____. *Hide or Seek.* Old Tappan, New Jersey: Fleming H. Revell Company, 1974.

Getz, Gene A. *Audiovisual Media in Christian Education.* Chicago: Moody Press, 1972.

Ginot, Haim. *Teacher and Child.* New York: Macmillan, 1972.

Hubbard, David. *Is the Family Here to Stay?* Waco: Word Books, 1971. (See especially chapter 6.)

McElrath, William N. *A Bible Dictionary for Young Readers.* Nashville: Broadman Press, 1965.

_____. *Bible Guidebook.* Nashville: Broadman Press, 1972.

Shedd, Charlie W. *Promises to Peter.* Waco: Word Books, 1970. (Part I is especially helpful.)

Check Yourself

1. Do you now have a program of enrichment and continuing

education (seminars, workshops, discussion, etc.) for teachers and leaders in your Sunday School?

2. As a department team, make plans for at least one enrichment opportunity for the coming year to help you improve your teaching and leading skills.

 **Appendix:
DEPARTMENT EVALUATION
FORM**

As a staff or individually, complete the following Evaluation Form as a first step for strengthening your Sunday School ministry. Complete those sections appropriate to your task.

Use the following numbers:
0—No
1 or 2—Seldom
3 or 4—Frequently
5—Always

I. GENERAL CONCERNS
A. Schedule

1. Does your schedule allow for frequent movement and variety of activities for your children? ____

2. Do you allow for at least some choice of Bible-related activities? ____

3. Do you include a brief time for worship? ____

4. Does your staff regularly evaluate the use of the Sunday School period?

B. Room Environment

1. Is your department neat and clean, colorful, light and warm? _____

2. Is your room adaptable for a variety of activities (small group, large group, etc.)? _____

3. Do you frequently change bulletin board displays and other visuals in your room to relate to unit aims and seasonal themes? _____

4. Are your supplies adequately organized, seeable, reachable and returnable? _____

5. Have you as a team evaluated your room environment? _____

II. FOR THE DEPARTMENT LEADER
A. Responsibilities

1. Do you consult with Sunday School and church officials about the needs of your department? _____

2. Do you schedule and lead your regular staff meetings to plan each unit of lessons? _____

3. Do you promote a team spirit and unit through building trust and affirming each staff member? _____

4. Are you available to be a spiritual leader and counselor for your staff members? _____

5. Do you provide enrichment opportunities for your staff members (workshops, seminars, etc.) and encourage them to participate? _____

6. Do you understand your specific responsibilities during Bible Study, Bible Sharing and Bible Learning Activities? _____

III. FOR THE TEACHER
A. Responsibilities

1. Do you understand your specific responsibilities during Bible Study, Bible Sharing and Bible Learning Activities? ___

2. Do you devote adequate time to careful preparation for each week's lesson? ___

3. Do you regularly attend departmental planning meetings? ___

4. Do you understand the importance of working with other staff members as a team? ___

5. Do you seek to establish relationships with each child through a variety of means? ___

6. Do you seek to be sensitive to the spiritual needs of children and remain available to guide them to become members of God's family? ___

7. Do you pray regularly for your students and for their families? ___

8. Do you seek to use a variety of creative methods to make Bible study interesting and meaningful to the needs of your children? ___

9. Do you seek to provide for differences in ability and background so that the learning is appropriate for each individual child? ___

10. Do you seek to use the Student Book as an integral part of each class session? ___

11. Do you find ways to motivate students to use the Student Book as a Bible Study resource throughout each week? ___

12. Do you participate in opportunities for enrichment and training (workshops, etc.)? ___

Where from Here?

Once you have completed this form, review the questions and your responses. Note areas you scored with a low number. Decide which ones you would like to change to strengthen your ministry with children. Then identify specific steps which you need to take to make these changes.

Areas I'd Like to Change	Steps to Achieve These Goals
1.	
2.	
3.	